POISONED OCEANS

Honor Head

Gareth Stevens
PUBLISHING

Please visit our website, **www.garethstevens.com**.
For a free color catalog of all our high-quality books,
call toll free 1-800-542-2595 or fax 1-877-542-2596.

Cataloging-in-Publication Data

Names: Head, Honor.
Title: Poisoned oceans / Honor Head.
Description: New York : Gareth Stevens Publishing, 2019. | Series: Totally toxic
| Includes glossary and index.
Identifiers: ISBN 9781538234945 (pbk.) | ISBN 9781538234952 (library bound)
Subjects: LCSH: Marine pollution--Juvenile literature.
| Marine ecology--Juvenile literature.
Classification: LCC GC1090.H43 2019 | DDC 363.739'4--dc23

First Edition

Published in 2019 by
Gareth Stevens Publishing
111 East 14th Street, Suite 349
New York, NY 10003

© 2019 Gareth Stevens Publishing

Produced for Gareth Stevens by Calcium
Editors: Sarah Eason and Honor Head
Designers: Paul Myerscough and Steve Mead

Photo credits: Cover: Shutterstock: SignatureMessage; Inside: Shutterstock: aldarinho:
p.43; Steve Allen: p. 26; Allexxandar: p. 14b; Andrey Armyagov: p. 10t; Ase:
pp. 40–41; Peter Asprey: p. 20b; Maxim Blinkov: p. 35; BMJ: p. 4b; Rich Carey:
p. 10b, p. 24, pp. 30l, 30b; Hung Chung Chih: p. 12; wim claes: p. 16; Cornelius:
p. 38; paul cowell: p. 17tl; curraheesgutter: p. 39r; Darkydoors: p. 29; Suriya Desatit:
p. 9t; Calvin Dexter: p. 4t; Marius Dobilas: p. 8; Annalisa e Marina Durante: p. 5t;
Gagliardimages: p. 33; Dana Gardner: p. 37b; Sait Ozgur Gedikoglu: p. 42; graf:
pp. 1, 7t; Kev Gregory: p. 34; Gwoeil: p. 31t; DMHal: p. 37t; hiphoto: p. 17tr; Danny
E Hooks: p. 19b; hxdyl: p.13t; Andrea Izzotti: p. 14t; kajornyot wildlife photography:
p. 22; Matej Kastelic: p. 18; Brian Kinney: p. 28; lazyllama: p. 5b; Masterphoto:
p. 36r; Vladimir Meinik: p. 25; Dudarev Mikhail: p. 6; Napat: p. 19t; Niar: p.15;
nicepix: p. 27t; pixfly: p. 36l; Andrey Popov: p. 32t; Ppl: p. 21; Fluke Samed: p. 20t;
Anna Segeren: pp. 14–15; Sunghorn: p. 7b; ssuaphotos: p. 11; Superjoseph: p. 40b;
Corepics VOF: p. 23; Bjoern Wylezich: p. 41.

Printed in the United States of America

CPSIA compliance information: Batch #CW19GS.
For further information contact Gareth Stevens, New York, New York, at 1-800-542-2595.

CONTENTS

CHAPTER 1

PLANET OCEAN

When you look at Earth from space, it looks blue. This is because around 70 percent of the earth is made up of oceans. The seas that cover our planet are vital to the health and well-being of all living things. Plants that live in the ocean produce more than half the oxygen that humans and animals need to breathe, and the oceans absorb dangerous gases from the air to keep it healthy.

Our planet looks blue because it is covered in water. About 70 percent of our oxygen is produced by the world's oceans.

The Water Cycle

Oceans are a vital part of the water cycle. This is the process by which water moves from the sea, to the air, and then back to the land. Billions of gallons of water evaporate from the surface of the oceans every day. The water forms a gas called water vapor in the air, turns into clouds, and falls again as rain. Rain helps us grow food to eat and gives life to trees. Trees help to maintain the health of our planet by absorbing poisonous carbon dioxide gases and releasing oxygen. In addition, trees give us many essentials, such as food, wood, and other materials that we use every day. Rain also keeps the earth's water levels stable, so that we have enough clean water to drink, for sanitation and industrial uses, such as for making electricity.

Rain falls to the earth.

The water becomes vapor and clouds.

Water evaporates from sea and land.

The water cycle ensures that people, animals, and plants have fresh water, and it helps control our climate.

Food for Thought

For thousands of years, oceans have been a vital source of food for humans. People in many countries rely on fish and seafood as an essential part of their daily diet. In recent years, seafood has become more popular worldwide, especially in the West, where it is now considered a healthy alternative to meat. A large percentage of seafood is also used as animal feed. But the oceans don't just feed us; we also use them to move vast amounts of products around the world. Nearly everything we eat, wear, use, and enjoy relies on the oceans.

Many people enjoy beach vacations, so they can have fun and keep cool.

This dark-colored toxic runoff is pouring straight into the ocean in Sri Lanka, Asia. Point source runoff comes from a known source, such as a factory or a hotel.

Seas Under Threat

We need healthy oceans to keep healthy ourselves, but our seas are now in danger. They are threatened by a constant flow of toxic chemicals and other waste products that combine to create a big stew of toxicity. Most countries have a variety of rivers, lakes, creeks, estuaries, and streams. These are waterways that we can see, but there is also a lot of water that we can't see, either above or below ground. Runoff is water that flows off the land and becomes part of the water cycle. Groundwater gathers under the ground.

Seasick

Runoff can seep into the ground and end up in lakes, streams, and finally, the ocean. Runoff can be rainwater and snowmelt. It can also be toxic water that is hazardous to wildlife and humans. Nonpoint source runoff comes from fields, roads, factories, mines, and housing. Our roads are clogged with cars, trucks, and bikes.

Each day, millions of vehicles drip oil onto our roads, which seeps into the ground. Chemicals such as nitrogen and phosphorous used in farm and garden fertilizers, and waste from animals on farms, join runoff. This all seeps into the soil and then into the waterways, then starts its journey to the sea. Wastewater from everyday activities at home, school, or work—such as taking a shower or flushing the toilet—creates wastewater that can become runoff and groundwater that leaks into the earth's waterways.

Sewage pumped straight into the ocean in coastal areas pollutes the water and can give us stomach bugs, ear infections, or skin rashes when we go swimming.

This drone is spraying liquid fertilizer over a rice field. In many countries, rice is the main source of the population's diet.

Fatal Fish Farms

The world's population is growing, and our seas are overfished. In many parts of the world, ocean fish stocks are so low that governments have banned fishing in some areas, in order to give the fish population time to breed and grow. All this means that there are not enough fish in our oceans to feed everyone, and in some seas, fish stocks have already run out.

An alternative to fishing in the open seas is fish farms. Here, hundreds of thousands of fish are kept tightly packed in round pens or cages. Each fish eats three to five times its own weight and can grow rapidly. But the result is that the food such as herring the farmed fish eat are now in danger of becoming scarce.

Fish farms are now common around the world. Among the species raised by fish farmers are trout, salmon, tilapia, cod, and catfish. They may be raised in freshwater or seawater.

Toxic Plateful

Fish farms use chemicals that can be harmful to other sea life as well as to humans. There are chemicals in the disinfectant that is used to keep the cages and surrounding water clean from fish waste. Other chemicals are used to keep the fish free from lice and other diseases that spread from fish to fish.

Recent reports from Southeast Asia have stated that illegal and toxic pesticides, such as endosulfan (which is banned in over 80 countries because it is so toxic), are being used in shrimp farms. The pesticides affect the whole aquatic food chain, which includes humans. The dangers to humans include brain damage, cancer, and other health issues. Some of these chemicals may stay in the environment for decades.

Farmed salmon are fed special additives to give them a deep orange-pink color. Without them, these salmon would have pale gray flesh. Wild salmon get their color from eating krill and shrimp.

WHO'S TO BLAME? THE TOXIC TRUTH

In 2017, pesticides used at salmon fish farms contaminated 45 lochs along the coastline of Scotland. Levels of chemicals used to kill the sea lice on the salmon had exceeded the safety limit by more than 100 times in the last 10 years. Environmentalists believe that chemical pollution is a "toxic time bomb." Many say that the Scottish Environment Protection Agency (SEPA) has been aware of the dangerous levels of pesticides being used for many years, and it has done nothing about it. So, who is to blame: SEPA, for ignoring the problem; the fish farmers, for using dangerous amounts of chemicals; or consumers, for demanding more salmon to eat and at cheaper prices? Think of a "for and against" argument for SEPA, the fish farmers, and consumers.

CHAPTER 2
OCEAN ECOSYSTEM

The ocean ecosystem includes millions of living things, such as bacteria, crustaceans, fish, birds, mammals, and plants. Nonliving things, such as the sun and rain, are also part of the ecosystem. Every part of the ocean ecosystem affects our lives, from our weather to the food we eat. Our oceans' ecosystems contain a wide variety of habitats, including the freezing polar Arctic ocean and warm tropical seas. Fishing provides work for more than 200 million people worldwide, and seafood is the main source of protein for more than 1 billion people.

Ocean habitats, such as this coral reef, contain the greatest range of living things to be found anywhere on Earth. Seaweed and aquatic plants provide food and shelter for fish and other sea animals.

Earth Needs Oceans

Our oceans absorb and store heat from the sun. All the oceans are connected by currents that constantly move around the world. Currents carry heat from the sun from one place to another and help regulate our weather and climate. The warm water heats the air above it, and this air is blown across the land, creating our climate. Ocean currents can also carry and spread toxins, garbage, and other pollutants that get into the oceans.

Our oceans help keep us alive. Aquatic plants growing in the oceans create more than half the oxygen that humans and other land animals need to live. The vast open waters absorb huge amounts of carbon dioxide, and this helps to keep the earth's temperature at a safe level. Nearly half the carbon dioxide produced by human activities in the last 200 years, such as air pollution from airplanes and heat from our homes, schools, and industries, has dissolved in the oceans. One of the biggest threats to oceans today is the increase in carbon dioxide that is found in air and water.

Exhaust fumes from traffic pollute the air. This pollution contains carbon dioxide, which is absorbed into the oceans where it can harm wildlife and damage the delicate ecosystems there.

Increasing Pollution

Since the Industrial Revolution of the nineteenth century, more than 200 years ago, humans have been burning fossil fuels such as coal and oil. The fuel is burned to generate power that is turned into electricity. The electricity powers factories and industries, which produce goods for us to buy. As the world population increases, more and more countries turn agricultural and rural land into factories. They try to meet the demand from consumers for goods, such as clothes, furniture, and electrical goods. The fuel needed to transport the goods by air, sea, or road also adds to the overall toxic pollution.

Greenhouse Gases

When fossil fuels burn, they release carbon dioxide into the air. Carbon dioxide is a greenhouse gas. This means that, along with other greenhouse gases, such as nitrous oxide, methane, and ozone, carbon dioxide traps heat from the sun in the air. The trapped gases act a little like a greenhouse that surrounds Earth, making our climate warmer and warmer. This is known as the Greenhouse Effect, and it is seriously damaging world environments, including our oceans.

As the air becomes warmer, the polar ice caps melt and sea levels rise. If this continues, many low-lying land areas will be flooded and whole communities made homeless. With climate change, some crops may not grow, causing food shortages. Wildlife and their habitats could be badly damaged and disappear.

In some countries, such as China, people wear masks to protect themselves from the toxic air. The pollution is caused by traffic, factories, and industry, such as coal mining.

Methane is produced by fossil fuels but also by rotting and decaying waste in landfill dumps.

WHO'S TO BLAME? THE TOXIC TRUTH

As people have more money to spend, they buy more and more things. This is called consumerism. There is a huge increase in consumer demand for the latest cars, clothes, toys, smartphones, game consoles, and everything else we think we need for a comfortable life. To make these things, more factories are needed, which pump more carbon dioxide into the air. In 2014, a report by the Intergovernmental Panel on Climate Change (IPCC) stated that emissions of carbon dioxide and other greenhouse gases grew twice as fast in the first decade of the twenty-first century as they did during the previous three decades, and much of that was due to burning more coal. But who is to blame? Is it the factories that produce the goods? Or, are we the consumers to blame for the never-ending demand for new bigger, better, faster goods, even when the ones we have are perfectly okay? How do you think we as consumers could help reduce levels of carbon dioxide?

This cormorant dives into the water to catch fish that have eaten krill, below. If one of these animals has become diseased by pollution, the disease will then be passed along the food chain.

Acid Attack

One effect of increased carbon in the air is the acidification of the oceans. The oceans already contain a certain amount of acid that combines with other natural chemicals in the sea to keep it at a stable level. But, as the oceans absorb more and more carbon dioxide, this reacts with other natural chemicals in the water to create higher levels of acid. This results in ocean acidification. This means that the oceans produce less calcium carbonate, which is essential to strengthen the protective shells of sea animals. If their shells become weak, the animals die. As a result, there is less food for the bigger fish, which damages the entire food chain—right up to humans. Calcium carbonate is also needed for the growth of coral.

Vital Links

There are many food chains in the varied habitats of the oceans. A food chain can be simple or complex, but it needs all the links of the chain in order to stay in place. If one link is broken, it can damage the whole chain. A simple food chain is one where marine plants feed plankton (tiny animals and plants), which feed fish, which then feed humans.

Polluted Food Chain

If plankton or fish die because of pollution, there is less food for humans. Toxic damage to the oceans hits hardest at the bottom of the food chain because toxins easily contaminate plankton. The toxic plankton are eaten by secondary consumers, such as fish, and then by primary consumers, such as whales, sharks, and humans. The poison moves all the way to the top of the food chain.

Fish store harmful toxins, such as mercury and lead, in their flesh, and when the fish are eaten, these toxins are passed on to the next link in the food chain. Each link eats more of the food beneath it. So, a human may only eat one tuna at a time, but a tuna will eat several small fish. Small fish may eat hundreds of plankton. As you move up the food chain, the deadly toxins increase from link to link.

Algae Threat

Along with killing off the food needed at the bottom of the food chain, warmer water encourages the growth of blue-green algae. The algae keep other plants from growing that are an important link at the beginning of the food chain. Research has shown that tiny organisms on the ocean floor could become extinct due to global warming and acidification. If they die, the whole food chain is threatened. Humans who eat fish as their main diet could face food shortages.

A shoal of small fish pick at tiny organisms on the ocean floor. If their food source is toxic and kills them, other animals further up the food chain will starve and die.

CHAPTER 3

OIL IN OUR OCEANS

Oil spills in our oceans make headlines. We've all seen news footage of oil slicks that trail for miles around a spill site, turning the ocean into a slick of toxic colors. Even worse to witness are the effects of an oil spill when it hits the coastline. Golden sand turns into a thick, black mess that smothers animal life and damages beaches.

Oil is a toxin. If it is consumed by a living organism, the toxin poisons it. When oil gets into seawater, it seeps into food chains and ecosystems, poisoning plant and animal life. Not only does oil poison, the sticky substance clings to fish and other marine animals, such as seals and dolphins.

The oil on seabirds clogs up their feathers, so that they can't fly, swim, or keep warm.

Poisoned sardines can harm other animals that eat them—including us, if they end up on our plates.

Dangerous and Deadly

Oil is like a deadly black glue—once it covers a bird or mammal, chances are that the creature will die if it is not cleaned quickly. An oil spill most likely spells death for any living things that come into contact with it.

In 2010, after an explosion on the *Deepwater Horizon* oil drilling platform, millions of barrels of oil poured into the Gulf of Mexico. The explosion killed 11 workers and caused an environmental disaster. Years later, large numbers of dolphins and turtles are still dying as a result of the oil spill accident.

WHO'S TO BLAME? THE TOXIC TRUTH

After the *Deepwater Horizon* oil spill of 2010, the US government held the company British Petroleum (BP) responsible. The government said that BP did not have the correct safety measures in place and had tried to save money at the expense of drilling safety. In a report issued in 2011, the government stated that the oil spill could easily happen again because of "absent significant reform in both industry practices and government policies ." Who do you think is to blame for oil pollution cases such as this, the oil companies or the governments that regulate them but did nothing to make sure rules were being followed ? Explain your thinking.

The largest tankers in the world are the Very Large Crude Carriers (VLCC) and the Ultra Large Crude Carriers (ULCC). These tankers carry about 3 million barrels of crude oil.

Environmental Disaster

Giant oil tankers, called "supertankers," move raw, unrefined oil that has been pumped straight out of the ground, across thousands of miles of ocean. The oil is taken to refineries on land, where it is processed into fuel and other oil-based products. The processed oil products are then transported by tanker across the ocean to the country where they will be sold. Most tankers transport their cargo safely, but when an accident happens, it means disaster for the environment.

Oil Time Bomb

In January 2018, the oil tanker *Sanchi* collided with a Chinese freighter just off the coast of Hong Kong. A mighty explosion resulted in thousands of tons of oil pouring into the ocean. The *Sanchi* was carrying about 1 million barrels of crude oil called natural gas condensate, which is used as jet fuel.

The remains of the *Sanchi* sank to the ocean floor and much of the oil was burned off by raging fires that followed. However, environmentalists say that the remaining cargo could be a "time bomb." If the condensate slowly leaks out, the ocean floor and surrounding wildlife will be affected for decades to come. One immediate impact would be on the rich fishing grounds where the accident happened, which is considered one of China's finest fishing resources. Light crude oil is more difficult to clean up than heavy crude oil, and condensate is highly toxic.

Black Beaches

In 2002, the structurally defective *Prestige* oil tanker broke in two off the coast of Spain. Its cargo of crude oil swamped the Spanish coastline, turning the beaches black for thousands of miles. The oil also reached beaches around Portugal and France. It was Spain's worst ecological disaster. The wreck continued to leak tons of oil every day. The hydrocarbons in the oil poisoned plankton, fish, fish eggs, crustaceans, sharks, birds, and much more in the delicate ecosystem. Fishing grounds were devastated, and all offshore fishing was banned by the government for six months.

Tiny plankton are one of the first links in the ocean food chain. These bottom-feeding creatures consume toxic oil, which is then passed along the food chain.

Spilled oil can be carried for miles by ocean currents to areas far away from the original accident.

Black Death

Birds and marine wildlife are usually fatally damaged by oil spills. When a bird's feathers are damaged by oil, the bird is at risk of dying from the cold, being unable to fly, and being poisoned from swallowing oil when it preens. These birds are in danger from predators because they can't fly away. The damage also means that they can't fly or dive for food, so they risk starvation and dehydration. Other sea animals can suffer from serious deformities due to oil pollution. Shrimp may be born without eyes and with holes in their shells.

All sea animals, big and small, can be badly damaged by oil spills. This crab is covered with oil.

This dolphin is swimming near some oil rigs. Small oil spills that build up in the ocean are harming dolphins.

Deadly Damage

Oil that is swallowed by birds can affect their digestive system: The bird can't process its food properly, so it becomes weak and dies in a very short time. Its beak and eyes can become ulcerated. Scientists believe kidney damage can develop as a result of the toxins in oil and dehydration. The oil may also affect future generations of birds. It can make eggs infertile and cause eggs to have thinner shells, so that they break before the chicks can hatch.

Sea Mammals

Animals that live in our oceans—such as dolphins, sea otters, sea lions, porpoises, and whales—can all be harmed by oil. Even polar bears and other large mammals at the top of the food chain can be affected. Polar bears, young sea lions, and sea otters can be affected if their fur becomes matted with oil. When the animals try to clean their fur, they may be poisoned. When dolphins and whales swim through oil slicks, their skin often becomes damaged.

Major internal injury can also be caused, including clogged lungs and kidney, liver, and brain damage. Sea otters that spend most of their time on the surface of the water, plus animals that have to come to the surface to breathe, are particularly at risk because this is where chemicals are at their most toxic.

The harm from oil spills is long-lasting and affects wildlife for generations. Whales and dolphins can be seriously harmed if they eat contaminated prey, breathe toxic chemicals, and swim through oil.

This dead dolphin has been washed up on the beach. It can take an environment up to six years or longer to recover from an oil spill.

This cleanup crew is using high-pressure hoses to suck up the oil from a spill as quickly as possible.

Quick Action

After a major oil disaster, immediate action is needed to keep the environmental damage to a minimum. A major cleanup may include rapid-response units from several different countries and environmental organizations, such as the Coast Guard and Environmental Protection Agency (EPA). When oil spills into water, it forms a thick slick that floats on the surface. The oil spreads out and becomes thinner and thinner. Speed is essential to keep the oil from being carried farther away on waves and currents.

Oil spills that result from an explosion might end in a fire that burns up the oil on the surface. Often, cleanup crews will set fire to oil spills to burn off the oil. However, oil fires create toxic smoke, so oil is not burned near coastal areas. When this happens, cleanup crews use large sponges that absorb oil from the water instead. Sometimes, an oil spill will be left untreated if it is not threatening wildlife or human habitation, because the waves, sun, and weather will break it down naturally.

Deadly Droplets

In tropical waters, oil spills are sometimes broken down with chemicals. This creates tiny oil droplets that are easily absorbed by marine life, poisoning the food chain. In a study scientists found that oil droplets are more toxic and damaging to coral reefs than the crude oil that is being cleaned up. The droplets caused rapid coral reef death and stunted growth.

Coastal oil spills can be more difficult to clean up, since they have an immediate impact on wildlife and habitats. Oiled beaches are sprayed with special substances that break down the oil. Big floats and balloons are used to keep birds and other wildlife away from the danger area.

Saving Wildlife

Wild birds become very stressed when handled by humans and washed. Expert wildlife organizations, such as International Bird Rescue, rush to the scene. Their highly trained staff first try to calm the birds, then wash them using special soap. When the birds' feathers are completely waterproof again, they are released back into the wild. It is much more difficult to capture and clean mammals such as seals, sea otters, manatees, and turtles, and little can be done to help dolphins, whales, and porpoises affected by oil slicks.

This guillemot is cleaned after an oil spill. Teams have to work fast to keep birds from swallowing any oil.

CHAPTER 4

COASTAL CRISIS

Polluted beaches can damage birds that feed along the coasts, such as wading birds and seagulls.

The area between the sea and the land is known as the coastal area. This can be a sandy beach, a rocky shoreline, a wetland, a mangrove forest, a coral reef, or an estuary. These coastal areas have a vital role to play in the health of our oceans and our everyday lives.

Each coastal habitat contributes to the overall health of the oceans. Seabirds use sheltered rocky coasts to breed and raise their young. Turtles live in the ocean all the time, but they return to the beach where they were born to lay eggs and produce the next generation of turtles. Some coastlines grow grasses with thick roots that help bind sand together to protect the shoreline from erosion. Wading birds use the seashore to hunt for fish. Wetlands can absorb damaging toxins before they reach the sea.

Safe Seas

Coastal areas are also great for humans. They provide beaches for vacations, rock pools to explore, and good opportunities for swimming. However, today, many of our coastal habitats are being poisoned. Heavy rains, especially after a long, dry period, can cause sewers to overflow and wash large quantities of farm and animal waste into coastal areas. Most countries have government guidelines that control the quality of seawater around vacation sites and beaches. They also have professional agencies that regularly monitor the quality of the seawater.

Toxic Tide

As the world population increases, there is mounting pressure for more houses to be constructed—and many people like to live near the coast. More and more coastline is being taken up by urbanization—the construction of houses, roads, schools, and hospitals. Urbanization not only destroys habitats forever, but toxic runoff and other building waste end up along the coastline. There, it poisons wildlife and destroys plant life. Eventually, human waste, sewage runoff, contaminated groundwater, and other wastewater add to the toxic mix found along the coasts.

In the Arctic, polar bears walk along a coastline littered with old and rusting garbage that pollutes the beach and spills into the ocean.

Acres of crops are regularly sprayed with fertilizer and pesticides, which release dangerous chemicals into the air and the soil.

Nutrient Overload

Nitrogen and phosphorous are nutrients that are essential to all forms of life, and they are part of the ocean's ecosystems. They help aquatic plants and algae to grow. Algae and marine plants provide food for fish, shellfish, and other small sea animals. However, too much of these nutrients can be very harmful.

Human activity has increased the amount of phosphorous and nitrogen found in seawater and air. These nutrients are found in farm and garden fertilizers, soap, detergents, and animal manure—and they are polluting our oceans. This is called nutrient pollution, and it can have serious consequences for both humans and wildlife. Nitrogen can produce toxic air gases, such as ammonia and ozone, that affect our breathing, create thick smog, and damage plant growth.

Bloom of Death

Too much nitrogen and phosphorous in water causes algae to grow faster than ecosystems can manage. Large growths of algae are called algal bloom, and these can have a devastating effect on wildlife. The bloom blocks out sunlight and keeps oxygen from reaching fish and other organisms in the water, causing them to suffocate. In some places, algal bloom has killed all the marine life, creating dead zones. A study by scientists in 2008 found 405 dead zones around the world. The toxins created by algal bloom can also affect humans who eat infected fish or shellfish, or drink the water.

In Thailand, this algal bloom has formed as a result of fish farming and farmers using too many chemicals on their land.

WHO'S TO BLAME? THE TOXIC TRUTH

In 2015, a massive algal bloom spread across the Pacific Ocean from Southern California to Alaska. Because the bloom was so long-lasting and so toxic, it contaminated the food chain, and several commercial fisheries along the West Coast had to close. It is thought that sudden rain showers washed nutrient-rich farm fertilizer into the unusually warm ocean water, triggering the bloom. The food chain was affected, and more than 50 sea lions along the Monterey coast became sick. It is difficult to say who is responsible for this kind of toxic activity when there is no specific culprit and when it is the result of a series of events. Do you think that global warming and the increased use of nutrient pollutants could result in more of this type of deadly outbreak? What can we do about it? Is there a better way to farm food?

Life and Color

Coral reefs are colorful, busy places with the widest range of marine life of all the ocean ecosystems. They are home to thousands of fish, shellfish, plants, turtles, mollusks, snails, and other sea animals that feed, hunt, and breed among the living coral. A coral reef is a living organism made up of billions of tiny animals called coral polyps, connected together. Each coral polyp has a hard outer skeleton made mainly from calcium carbonate. Some reefs are millions of years old, but they are very fragile and need warm water and sunlight to grow and thrive.

Human activity is putting a huge strain on the world's reefs. Divers and snorkelers often damage and break delicate coral. Pleasure boats and fishing trawlers destroy the coral by bulldozing over it or damaging it with propellers and blades. Toxic pollution damages the coral and the reef wildlife.

Polyps contain algae that give them their colors, such as pink and purple, as well as nutrients that the coral needs to stay alive.

Toxic Trio

Coral reefs are being badly damaged by global warming, ocean acidification, and pollution. As seas become warmer, the coral is becoming bleached. The algae that live inside the coral (and give the coral its amazing colors) begin to die off. The coral then turns ghostly white. Once bleaching happens, the whole reef soon dies. Toxic runoff or acid rain increases ocean acidification, which weakens and eventually dissolves the shell that supports the coral. This destroys the reef. The shells of crustaceans that live on the reef are also damaged from acidification. Pollution from land runoff and groundwater—such as human waste, disinfectants, and sewage from hotels and tourist resorts—can cause algal bloom, which suffocates the living corals and poisons the water nearby.

Oil spills can also be catastrophic, damaging the coral and poisoning fish and other sea animals. As well as infecting the food chain, it can take decades for a reef to recover from an oil spill.

Rising temperatures kill the coral, turning the reef into a white, bleached wilderness where little or no sea life can survive.

DUMPING GROUNDS

Oceans are deep and vast, and for many centuries, people believed that trash dumped in the oceans would just dissolve or sink to the bottom. Today, we know that ocean tides, currents, and winds carry toxic waste around the world, and that it lasts for hundreds of years. Most of the stuff that is dumped in oceans is toxic or becomes toxic. In time, barrels split and the contents leak out, plastic breaks down into life-threatening components, and garbage injures and kills wildlife.

Dumped human garbage is seriously damaging the oceans and the living things that they support.

Radioactive Waste

Nuclear reactors or power plants are huge machines that release energy to create electricity. The metal uranium is used to help release the energy. Nuclear electricity is considered clean energy, since it doesn't pollute the air or produce greenhouse gases. But it is a complicated process that requires top-level safety measures at all stages in order to avoid highly toxic explosions or spills. Making nuclear energy results in radioactive waste. This is seriously harmful to all forms of life and must be securely contained for hundreds of years until the waste has reached safe levels.

Deadly Dumping

From 1946 to 1993, countries that had nuclear power dumped radioactive waste in the oceans. This has resulted in a serious threat to the environment, since containers could decay and radioactive materials seep into the water. Currents could then carry the waste around the world or help it rise to the surface. In 1993, an international agreement between the countries that produced nuclear waste banned the dumping of the waste in the oceans. However, tons of radioactive material are already there, and we have little way of knowing what effect they may have on our oceans over the coming decades.

If the contents of barrels full of nuclear waste spill out, it could result in an environmental disaster that would last for generations.

Dumping Sewage

Land-based pollution makes up 44 percent of the total pollution in the oceans. This includes sewage, urban and agricultural runoff, mining waste, oil spills, and dumping garbage in the ocean. Toxic air pollution, such as acid rain, accounts for another 33 percent. Only 12 percent of toxic pollution actually originates from activities at sea. Some of the most hazardous things that are dumped in our oceans are human sewage and wastewater from toilets, baths, showers, and dishwashing. A lot of this wastewater finds its way into the oceans.

Things that we do at home, such the laundry, cause wastewater runoff that ends up in the oceans.

WHO'S TO BLAME? THE TOXIC TRUTH

Barbados has a sewer crisis. At the beginning of 2018, raw effluent began to leak from manholes in the roads, reaching beaches and the ocean along popular coastal tourist areas. The country's sewage system is old and inadequate for its growing population and tourist industry. The majority of residents are not connected to a centralized sewage system, but instead use local on-site wastewater treatments, which are unable to manage pollutants such as nitrogen. A lot of waste from older homes is disposed of into the ground and ends up in the ocean as runoff. As a result of the pollution, many tourists have complained about getting sick.

The head of the Barbados Water Authority (BWA) said they first identified this as a potential problem in 2017, but politicians deny that they knew about the problem. Experts say that the original sewage plant is just a filter and not a real sewage treatment plant, so untreated sewage can end up in the ocean. So, who is to blame—politicians for not providing enough funds to update the system or the BWA for building an inadequate plant in the first place? Who needs to take action, and why?

Cruise Control

Many cruise ships use up-to-date sewage recycling systems to ensure that nothing toxic ends up in the oceans. However, a report by Friends of the Earth (an environmental campaigning organization) in 2016 found that almost 40 percent of ships they surveyed still used outdated waste treatment technology. The sewage that poured from these ships into the oceans contained high levels of human waste matter, bacteria, and other poisonous contaminants.

Supersized cruise ships carrying thousands of passengers create tons of waste on each cruise.

Killing Wildlife

From the very tops of mountains to the depths of the oceans, our planet is becoming a huge garbage dump. One of the most deadly types of trash is plastic. Over 8 million tons of plastic is dumped in our oceans every year. Plastic kills and injures animals in many ways. Some mistake plastic garbage, such as plastic bags, for food and eat it. This causes internal injuries and blockages that can lead to a painful death and starvation.

Over 90 percent of all seabirds have plastic pieces in their stomachs. Other wildlife becomes tangled in discarded plastic, such as plastic fishing nets. Plastic six-pack rings or yokes can get stuck around the necks of birds and other smaller sea animals. This chokes them to death or keeps them from swimming or flying. Plastic snags on coral and damages it. Forty percent of the garbage in our oceans is plastic, and is doing untold damage to wildlife.

This seal has gotten tangled up in plastic fishing nets. This stops the seal from swimming and hunting, and it will die of starvation.

Toxic Food Chain

Plastic can take hundreds of years to degrade and disappear, but scientists have discovered that plastic can dissolve faster in the ocean, and this is creating new problems. As plastic decomposes in the water, it starts giving out toxins that are potentially dangerous to human and animal life. Plastic is now becoming a deadly source of chemical pollution in our oceans.

Chemicals such as bisphenol and styrene monomer, found in plastic bottles and food packaging, can keep animals from breeding properly and can cause cancer. Styrofoam and other plastics break down into tiny pieces called "nurdles." These soak up other chemicals in the ocean and become highly toxic. They sink to the bottom of the ocean, and huge amounts are washed up on shores around the world.

Marine wildlife, such as this turtle, often get tangled up in plastic garbage, causing serious harm and death.

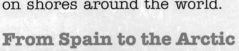

From Spain to the Arctic

Nurdles are eaten by jellyfish and other marine life, and so get into the food chain. As one animal eats another, the chemicals build up in the chain. This is potentially fatal for land animals, such as polar bears, and for humans, who are at the top of the food chain. Toxic chemicals in some plastics include lead, cadmium, and mercury. These toxins have been found in many fish in the ocean and are dangerous to humans who eat the polluted fish.

The once-pure Arctic Ocean is now becoming clogged with plastic. Tides carry the trash to the Arctic, where it floats on top of the ocean and is trapped in ice. A plastic butter tub was found in the Arctic; it had come from Spain. Local fishermen are concerned that plastic toxicity could poison fish.

Plastic water bottles can be recycled to create amazing sculptures, such as this large elephant.

Less Plastic, Please

What we dump in the ocean will stay there for generations to come. Some forms of plastic last for hundreds of thousands of years without decomposing. Governments and individuals have to work together to reduce the amount of garbage that ends up in the oceans. Most countries have laws to stop illegal dumping in oceans and elsewhere, and laws for the safe disposal of toxic waste. Many industries send their waste to other countries—especially developing countries—to be disposed of. Here, waste disposal standards may not be as high as those in the developed world.

Experts are looking at ways to reuse deadly garbage. One organization called Project Kaisei is researching ways to turn marine plastic trash into fuel. Many countries and communities are trying to ban or reduce the use of plastic bags. Only 15 percent of the world's plastic is recycled. Much of the plastic that is used to package goods is not recyclable. Environmentalists are urging manufacturers to use recyclable plastic in their packaging. This encourages the plastics industry to create better, recyclable plastic.

Get Creative

In some developing countries, local communities and individuals are finding ways to recycle plastic and other waste to make useful everyday items, such as flip-flops and schoolbags. In the United States, 4Ocean, now a global movement, was begun by two surfers who were appalled at the amount of garbage in our oceans. They organize "crews" around the world to clean the oceans and coasts of garbage and then recycle it into bracelets for sale, with all profits going back into the project.

Make a Difference

We can all make a difference. The majority of plastic in the oceans comes from the land: it is dumped on the streets, spilled from domestic garbage cans, or blown off landfill. Try to buy goods in recyclable plastic or no plastic at all. Throw your plastic away securely; for example, always cut plastic six-pack rings from cans and bottles before you recycle them. Tie plastic bags into knots, so they are not easily blown around. Put your litter in the garbage can, and recycle when you can.

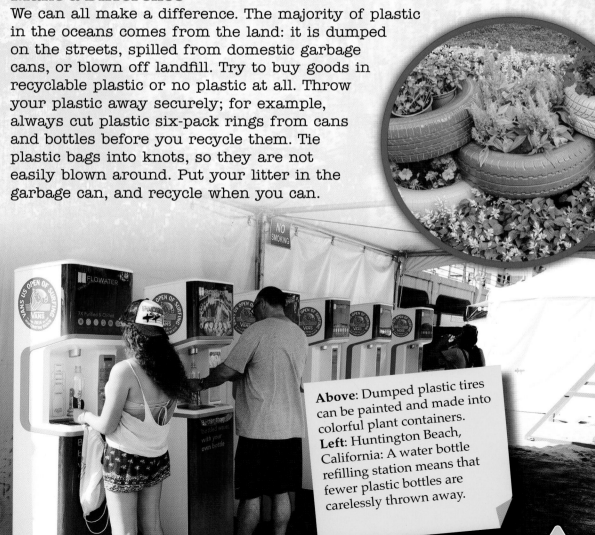

Above: Dumped plastic tires can be painted and made into colorful plant containers.
Left: Huntington Beach, California: A water bottle refilling station means that fewer plastic bottles are carelessly thrown away.

CHAPTER 6

MINING THE OCEAN

The sea around the Indonesian island of Bangka has been mined for tin for decades. The tin is used in circuit boards, smartphones, and tablets. To find it, land is bulldozed, destroying farms and forests. The land is then hosed down and dug up. This means that topsoil is washed away, and acidic soil comes to the surface, which is washed into the ocean. Miners then dredge the ocean floor looking for tin in the sand. Tin mining has made many people wealthier, but it has also caused human injuries, damaged ocean wildlife, killed fish stocks, and destroyed coral reefs.

In Alaska, dredgers that are used to mine for gold on the ocean floor damage the ocean environment.

Oil Drilling

Oil is essential to our lives. It is turned into electricity to power lights and machines, such as computers, washing machines, and dishwashers. It is used as fuel for cars, trucks, ships, and planes. It is also used to make plastic. Oil is a fossil fuel that is found deep underground, so drilling equipment is used to reach it on land and at sea, disturbing the environment and wildlife.

WHO'S TO BLAME? THE TOXIC TRUTH

One of Australia's worst oil disasters happened at the West Atlas oil drilling rig in the Timor Sea off the northern coast of Australia. From August to November 2009, oil leaked into the ocean. An oil slick of more than 2,300 square miles (5,956 sq km) wide formed. It did minimal damage to the Australian coast, but it had a major impact on the poor fishing communities of Indonesia.

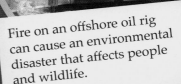

Fire on an offshore oil rig can cause an environmental disaster that affects people and wildlife.

In 2015, a report by the Australian Lawyers Alliance documented reports of sick and dying marine life in the area, including dead whales. Indonesian fishermen said that the oil reached their waters, killing thousands of fish, damaging their seaweed farms, destroying mangroves that protect their communities from flooding, and causing skin diseases. The estimated cost of the loss to fish and seaweed farming is believed to be about $1.2 billion per year since 2009.

The oil rig operators PTTEP Australasia, based in Perth, accepted full responsibility for the spill and paid fines to the Australian government. In 2010, the Indonesian government requested compensation for farmers, but up to 2015, nothing had been paid by PTTEP. The Australian government seems unwilling to help. Why do you think the government should get involved? Whose responsibility is it, and why?

The Final Frontier

Sand in shallow areas of the ocean has been mined for decades to make concrete and asphalt for use in construction. Mining for diamonds, gold, tin, and other precious stones is also common along the world's coasts. Today, discoveries of precious metals in the deepest parts of the ocean mean that mining companies want to extend their operations there, too.

Many environmentalists and ocean scientists think that deep-sea mining is a serious new threat to our oceans. Scientists have only explored about 5 percent of the world's oceans, so very little is known about the ecosystems and life-forms at some of the deepest levels. If drilling takes place, it is likely that deep-water habitats will be destroyed before scientists have a chance to explore and understand them.

Deep in the ocean, it is pitch-black and freezing cold, and the water pressure is very high. We know very little about the fish that live there.

Huge mining companies are racing to dig up precious deep-sea metals such as copper, gold, and silver.

Deep-Sea Discoveries

The deep-sea level begins at about 656 feet (200 m) down. Sunlight can't reach the deep ocean, so there is no plant life. Many of the organisms that live there make their own light using a method called bioluminescence. Recent deep-level exploration has only been possible because of the development of deep-sea submersibles. These are small craft that can travel many miles down into the ocean to gather water and sand samples, and they also take movies and photographs.

Scientists believe that organisms have evolved two particular characteristics to help them adapt to deep-sea life. These are gigantism (growing to a huge size) and living a very long life, sometimes for decades or even centuries. Most deep-sea animals brought to the surface die quickly because they are not adapted to life there, and scientists don't know how to keep them alive.

Hydrothermal vents are a recent deep-sea discovery. These are a little bit like mini volcanoes. They are found on the ocean floor and produce copper, gold, silver, zinc, and other valuable metals. Minerals such as copper, cobalt, and nickel have also been found in the deep ocean.

Giant tube worms, similar to these on a coral reef, have been discovered at the bottom of the ocean.

More Destruction

We have already done untold damage to our oceans, and deep-sea mining would lead to more, with thousands of miles of ocean bed being drilled and dredged. Exploring the deep ocean floor is like investigating another planet—we don't know what amazing scientific discoveries might be made.

Mining will mean deep-sea drilling into the ocean bed and dredging the ocean floor. Food chains and habitats will be damaged by mining equipment and possible oil spills. Chemicals released into the sea may be fatal or seriously injure deep-sea life. Dredging will raise huge amounts of sediment from the seafloor, which could smother fragile sea life and reduce habitats.

One of the fascinating discoveries made by scientists exploring the ocean depths is an ecosystem that relies on toxic gases. They found giant tube worms over 6 feet (2 m) tall that live on hydrogen sulfide. This gas is toxic to animals. Mining activity could release more of the lethal gas into other parts of the ocean, threatening marine wildlife and food chains at higher ocean levels.

A Better Way

Our oceans are precious and in danger. Governments and industry must think about more sustainable ways to produce the things we need, in ways that help to protect our oceans from further destruction. There are options. Energy can be made from renewable sources, such as solar and wind power. Refuse-derived fuel (RDF) can be made by sorting garbage to extract waste that can be made into energy pellets. The pellets can then be used at power plants.

Working Together for Our Oceans

Governments can make sure that mining operators follow strict rules and regulations and that the illegal dumping of waste carries heavy penalties. Governments should consult with marine experts before they allow mining companies to damage the deep-sea oceans forever. Farmers and gardeners can think about not using toxic fertilizers, pesticides, and insecticides. Each one of us can make small changes that could make a big difference to our oceans. Dispose of garbage properly, and check packaging for sustainably fished food. The ocean and its amazing wildlife needs all of us to look after it.

Governments and individuals have to find ways to make sure that garbage dumping in and around our oceans is stopped.

BE AN ECO REPORTER!

We have seen how plastic can damage our oceans by injuring and killing wildlife and leaking toxic chemicals into the water. So, what can you do about this? Research and report it!

① Research the Toxic Facts

- Search online for a stretch of coastline that has been badly polluted by plastic garbage.

- What are the causes of the pollution along the coast?

- Has fishing or swimming been affected by the pollution? How?

- Have the local people or governments done anything to reduce the amount of waste that enters the ocean? If so, what?

- How have food chains in the area been affected? How has the plastic disturbed the food chain and caused toxins to pass along it?

Report the Toxic Truth

Send a report about your findings to a local politician or council group, and ask them to stop the dumping of plastic in the ocean. Use the points below to help you construct your report:

- What facts can you use to support your findings about plastic pollution?

- What suggestions can you give to stop the dumping of plastic along the coastline? For example, many coastal communities form cleanup teams to remove plastic garbage from the beach. The trash can be turned into sculptures. What other ideas do you have to encourage people to clean up beaches?

- Describe your findings about how food chains are affected by plastic pollution. Show your research in a diagram of a food chain. Use labels and captions to explain your discoveries.

- Give suggestions on how you think the food chain could be protected.

SPREAD THE WORD

Remember, we all have a responsibility to protect our oceans. Tell your family and friends what you have learned about poisoned oceans and what they can all do to help protect these precious environments.

GLOSSARY

algae Tiny plantlike organisms that live in the water and are food for fish and some sea mammals.

bacteria Tiny organisms that can be seen only with a microscope.

carbon dioxide A colorless and odorless gas created when fossil fuels are burned.

climate The weather in a certain area over a period of time.

contaminated Infected or polluted with something.

crustaceans Shellfish such as shrimp and lobsters.

current A movement of water from one place to another.

dehydration Not having enough water in the body.

dredging Clearing something by digging or scooping it up.

ecological disaster A disaster for living things and their surroundings.

effluent Liquid sewage.

emissions Discharges such as poisonous gases from burning fuel.

environmentalists People who campaign to keep the environment safe and protected.

erosion When something is gradually worn away.

fossil fuels Fuels, such as gas and oil, made up of the remains of dead organisms over millions of years.

hydrocarbons A combination of hydrogen and carbon that occurs in natural gas and coal.

infertile Unable to produce offspring.

krill A tiny animal found at the bottom of food chains.

lice Small wingless insects that live on other animals.

methane A colorless, odorless hydrocarbon gas, part of natural gas.

mineral A solid substance, such as gold, that is found in the ground.

mollusk An invertebrate (an animal that does not have a backbone) that lives in damp or ocean habitats.

organism A living thing including plants and animals.

pesticides Chemicals sprayed on crops and plants to keep insects and other pests from causing damage.

plankton Microscopic living things, such as animals and plants, at the bottom of the food chain.

polar ice caps Large areas of layers of ice in the Arctic and Antarctica.

preens Preening is when a bird cleans its feathers.

sanitation The provision of clean drinking water and proper sewage disposal.

toxic Something that is poisonous and can harm and kill.

ulcerated To form ulcers or sores.

unrefined oil The form oil takes before it has been processed, also called crude oil.

FOR MORE INFORMATION

Books

Cousteau, Philippe, and Cathryn Berger Kaye. *Make a Splash!: A Kid's Guide to Protecting Our Oceans, Lakes, Rivers, & Wetlands*. Minneapolis, MN: Free Spirit Publishing, 2012.

Jakubiak, David J. *What Can We Do about Oil Spills and Ocean Pollution?* (Protecting Our Planet). New York, NY: PowerKids Press, 2011.

Kallen, Stuart A. *Trashing the Planet: Examining Our Global Garbage Glut*. Minneapolis, MN: Twenty-First Century Books, 2017.

Pfiffikus editors. *Water, Water Everywhere! Stop Pollution, Save Our Oceans* (Conservation for Kids: Children's Conservation Books). Pfiffikus, 2016.

Websites

www.marinemammalcenter.org
Learn how the Marine Mammal Center helps to rescue and conserve ocean wildlife.

www.nationalgeographic.com/environment/oceans/...
Find out how you can make a difference to the health of the oceans.

thankyouocean.org/kid-zone
Discover activities and videos to help your awareness of our amazing oceans.

www.greenpeace.org/usa/oceans
Check out what U.S. Greenpeace is doing to save oceans and fight ocean pollution.

oceanservice.noaa.gov/kids
Read more about ocean pollution, with activities and special resources for kids.

Publisher's note to educators and parents: Our editors have carefully reviewed these websites to ensure that they are suitable for students. Many websites change frequently, however, and we cannot guarantee that a site's future contents will continue to meet our high standards of quality and educational value. Be advised that students should be closely supervised whenever they access the Internet.

INDEX